COOKBOOK ON WELLNESS

Delicious quick and easy low-fat recipes

TABLE OF CONTENTS

INTRODUCTION	4
Where does the feeling of wellness come from?	4
WELLNESS RECIPES	6
FAST ZUCCHINI BUFFERS	6
SPINACH DUMPLINGS	7
WILD GARLIC PESTO	9
AVOCADO SPREAD	10
BANANA BREAD	11
ASPARAGUS SOUP	13
HUMMUS	15
SALMON STEAK	16
CLASSIC CUCUMBER SALAD	17
SUGAR SNAP	18
CLASSIC CUCUMBER SALAD	19
VEGAN BREAD DUMPLINGS	20
RICE SOUP	22
ZUCCHINI NOODLES	23
ZUCCHINI - POTATO CASSEROLE	24
POTATOES FROM THE STEAMER	25
TZATZIKI	26
KOHLRABI SALAD WITH APPLES	27
RASPBERRY SMOOTHIE	28
FRIED CHANTERELLES	29
CAULIFLOWER CASSEROLE	30
BREADED ZUCCHINI	31
RATATOUILLE	33
PUMPKIN SPAETZLE	34
STYRIAN AVOCADO SPREAD	36
PIKEPERCH FILLET WITH VEGETABLES	37
SIMPLE PUMPKIN SOUP	39
VITAL SALAD	40
COLESLAW	42

STINGING NETTLE SPINACH	43
TURKEY ROULADE	44
ZUCCHINI SOUP	45
PASTA WITH GREEN ASPARAGUS AND PROSCIUTTO	47
CELERY CREAM SOUP	48
FRIED RICE	49
CHICKEN WITH STIR-FRIED VEGETABLES IN SOY SAUCE	51
EGG SOUP	52
PEA PUREE	53
MEDITERRANEAN PASTA SALAD WITH OLIVE DRESSING	54
INDIAN LENTIL STEW	56
STUFFED ZUCCHINI	58
CHICKPEA AND ZUCCHINI PATTIES	59
BAKED AUBERGINES (AUBERGINES)	61
FRIED SALMON FILLETS	63
FRUIT SALAD FOR CHILDREN	64
NETTLE SOUP	65
OATMEAL MUESLI	66
GRILLED FENNEL	67
GREEN ASPARAGUS AU GRATIN	68
CARROT AND ZUCCHINI FRITTERS	70
MILLET BREAKFAST	71
CLASSIC ASPARAGUS	72
LINGUINE WITH ASPARAGUS	74
TOMATO SPREAD	75

INTRODUCTION

It is interesting to relate what we eat to mood and wellness. This opens up the possibility of providing our body with everything it needs to build inner joy and a sense of satisfaction in life. The wellness diet advises us to eat a balanced diet where we include some foods that can bring more joy and vigor to our lives.

Where does the feeling of wellness come from?

There is a substance called serotonin, or 5-HT, which behaves like a hormone in the blood and acts as a neurotransmitter in the brain. In this way, brain neurons use it to influence each other. Serotonin is directly related to our mood according to numerous studies.

The human body produces it from tryptophan, which is an essential amino acid. This means that the body cannot synthesize this amino acid on its own but must be ingested through the diet.

If the body wants to produce serotonin, it seems logical that we should provide it with all the tryptophan it needs to do so.

In addition to tryptophan there are many nutrients that are beneficial for our nervous system such as magnesium, vitamins, essential fatty acids ...

Eating a balanced diet is essential to maintain good health. You need to be very moderate alcohol, very sugary foods, trans fats, processed foods, refined flour, etc. The excesses in the feeding are not recommended and the monodietas can cause many deficiencies of nutrients

Some foods that can provide us with good levels of tryptophan and nutrients for our wellness:

- Nuts: good source of serotonin and Omega 3. Nuts contain appreciable amounts of tryptophan; but they are natural or toasted, not fried, etc.

- Banana: rich in magnesium and tryptophan.

- Seeds: pumpkin, sesame, sunflower, chia, flax seeds ... contain large amounts of minerals such as magnesium, vitamins, tryptophan, omega 3, omega 6 ...

- Legumes: contain a large amount of essential amino acids.

- Avocado: it has a large amount of essential amino acids, including tryptophan, as well as mineral vitamins that promote the synthesis of serotonin. It is a great ally of the nervous system.

- Honey: large number of enzymes and minerals. Antibacterial and sedative properties. Increases serotonin levels. Important is that the honey is organic without added sugars.

- Strawberries, blueberries, raspberries, blackberries: they contain a large number of antioxidants that prevent the oxidation of other molecules. They also prevent oxidative stress and reduce free radicals.

- Cocoa and dark chocolate (above 70%): contains chemicals that improve attention and the feeling of wellness such as caffeine and theobromine. Rich in magnesium, which is itself a muscle relaxant and is involved in the conversion of tryptophan into serotonin. We also find phenylethylamine in chocolate, which is a stimulating molecule similar to amphetamine.

- Griffonia: it is a plant native to Africa that its seeds offer high concentrations of 5-HTP, which is the precursor of serotonin and melatonin. It is found on the market as a food supplement in tablets that usually add magnesium and B 3 to optimize the synthesis of serotonin and melatonin. It is not recommended to take in combination with selective serotonin reuptake inhibitors (SSRIs) or monoamine oxidase inhibitors (MAOIs).

- Salmon and oily fish: they offer us Omega 3, vitamin B 12 and B 6, minerals such as selenium, magnesium and calcium. It is important to know that the B vitamins are necessary for the synthesis of serotonin. In fact, the presence of omega 3 in the blood has been associated with increased production of serotonin.

- Cheese, yogurt and kefir, preferably goat, can also provide us with interesting amounts of tryptophan, minerals and vitamins that favor the synthesis of serotonin.

- Egg: we find good concentrations of tryptophan and other essential amino acids, a large amount of minerals and vitamins. Organic eggs would be preferable.

- Turkey: provides us with good amounts of tryptophan, fatty acids, high content of iron and vitamins of group B.

WELLNESS RECIPES
FAST ZUCCHINI BUFFERS

Ingredients for 4 servings

- 600 G Zucchini (grated, small)
- 2 Pc Onion, small
- 2 Pc Garlic cloves
- 2 Pc Eggs
- 200 G oatmeal
- 70 G Cheese (grated)
- 1 prize salt
- 1 prize pepper
- 1 prize Basil (fresh or dried)
- 100 ml Bona oil

time

20 min. Total time 15 min preparation time 5 min.cooking & resting time

preparation

First, coarsely grate the peeled zucchini. Peel onion and garlic and chop finely.

Then mix the zucchini, onion, garlic, oat flakes and the grated cheese well in a bowl.

Then stir the eggs into the mixture and season well with salt, pepper and basil.

Then heat oil or butter in a pan and add the zucchini mixture as a pile into the hot oil and flatten it a little.

Fry the pancakes on both sides for 4-6 minutes each until they are golden brown, remove from the pan and drain on kitchen paper.

SPINACH DUMPLINGS

Ingredients for 4 servings

- 1 TL Butter for roasting the onion
- 2 Tbsp Flour

- 1 Pc Onion (small)
- 2 Pc Eggs (S)
- 125 ml milk
- 350 G Bread cubes
- 1 prize salt
- 750 G Spinach leaves (frozen, thawed)

Ingredients for serving

- 3rd Tbsp grated parmesan
- 1 TL butter

time

60 min. Total time 35 min preparation time 25 min. cooking & resting time

preparation

For the spinach dumplings, first defrost the spinach and cut it finely. You can of course also use fresh spinach. Cook this first. Squeeze the spinach well. Let freshly cooked spinach cool down to lukewarm.

Now finely chop the onion and fry in butter until translucent, leave to cool.

Now mix the bread cubes with the egg, milk, spinach, roasted cold onion and a little salt.

Add the flour to the dumpling mixture and form dumplings with wet hands. If the dough is too soft, add a little more flour. Let the mass steep briefly. Soak in gently surging salt water and let steep for about 15 minutes.

Serve the spinach dumplings sprinkled with brown butter (melt the butter until it is brown) and grated Parmesan.

WILD GARLIC PESTO

Ingredients for 4 servings

- 1 TL pepper
- 140 G Wild garlic
- 1 Cup Sunflower or pine nuts
- 1 prize salt
- 250 ml Bona olive oil

time

20 min. Total time 20 min preparation time

preparation

Wash the wild garlic, cut into small pieces, shake dry and layer in a shallow bowl.

Lightly roast the sunflower seeds in a pan without fat, then chop them up with a knife, place on the wild garlic and season with salt and pepper.

Then add the olive oil and stir well - if you like the pesto very fine, you can puree the mixture with the fine hand blender.

Finally, pour into clean, hot-rinsed screw-top jars and, depending on the consistency, add a little oil.

AVOCADO SPREAD

Ingredients for 4 servings

- 2   Pc   Avocados
- 4th Pc   Garlic cloves
- 1   Pc   lemon
- 1   Pc   onion
- 1   prize pepper
- 1   prize salt

time

70 min. Total time 10 min preparation time 60 min.cooking & resting time

preparation

Peel the avocado and remove the stone. Then puree with the juice of the lemon in a blender.

Finely chop the onion and fold in together with the finely chopped garlic. Season with salt and pepper. Let it steep in the refrigerator for 1 hour.

BANANA BREAD

Ingredients for 6 servings

- 1 Pk baking powder
- 3rd Pc Bananas, soft
- 160 G brown cane sugar
- 3rd Pc Eggs
- 0.125 l Light milk
- 150 G margarine
- 1 prize salt

- 100   G   Walnuts
- 350   G   Whole wheat flour
- 1   Tbsp   Fat for the shape

time

90 min. Total time 20 min preparation time 70 min.cooking & resting time

preparation

In a bowl, stir the soft margarine with the sugar until frothy. Then gradually add the eggs and stir well.

Now roughly mash the bananas with a fork and stir into the egg mass.

Then mix the flour with the baking powder, salt and the chopped nuts and stir alternately with the milk into the banana mixture.

Pour the dough into a well-greased loaf pan (approx. 1 3/4 l content). Bake in the preheated oven for about 1 hour at 180 ° top and bottom heat.

Let the banana bread cool in the tin for 10 minutes and then turn it out.

ASPARAGUS SOUP

Ingredients for 4 servings

- 60   G   butter or margarine
- 1   prize   grated nutmeg
- 60   G   Flour
- 0.25   l   Milk (low fat)
- 100   ml   Obers
- 1   prize   salt
- 500   G   asparagus
- 0.75   l   water

time

50 min. Total time 15 min preparation time 35 min.cooking & resting time

preparation

For the asparagus soup, first clean the asparagus and cook in boiling water with the addition of 2 teaspoons of salt and 1 teaspoon of sugar, depending on the thickness of the asparagus, for about 17-20 minutes until crisp and soft.

Remove the asparagus, let it cool down a little and then cut into smaller pieces (you can also use asparagus leftovers from the day before for the soup).

This is how the asparagus stock is ready (we'll need it soon).

To prepare the asparagus soup, first melt the butter in a larger saucepan.

Pull the pot off the stove.

Stir the flour into the melted butter with a mixing spoon and deglaze with about 3/4 liter asparagus stock, stirring well with the whisk so that no lumps are formed.

Salt the soup or season with stock cubes to taste.

Let the soup boil slowly for 15 minutes, this will make it lose its floury taste.

Pour in the milk, bring to the boil, then season.

If the soup is too thin, depending on your taste, you can thicken the soup with 1 teaspoon of cornstarch, which you stir into the cream. Otherwise just stir in the cream at the end and heat the asparagus pieces in the soup.

At the end, season with a little freshly grated nutmeg or a little white pepper.

HUMMUS

Ingredients for 4 servings

- 250   G   Chickpeas
- 2   Pc   Garlic cloves
- 1   prize   Caraway seed
- 1   TL   Paprika powder
- 1   Federation   Parsley, chopped
- 6th   Tbsp   Bona oil
- 1   prize   salt
- 50   ml   Lemon juice
- 4th   Tbsp   Sesame paste, tahini

time

80 min. Total time 20 min preparation time 60 min.cooking & resting time

preparation

Soak the chickpeas in cold water overnight.

Drain well and cook for 1 hour until soft, then pour off the water and set aside.

Peel and chop the garlic and mix with caraway seeds, paprika, chopped parsley, olive oil and salt. Stir in the chickpeas and puree well.

Finally stir in the tahini and lemon juice and put the mixture in the fridge.

SALMON STEAK

Ingredients for 4 servings

- 4th   Pc   Salmon steak
- 400   G   Cherry tomatoes
- 2   Pc   Onion, small
- 1   Federation   basil
- 2   Tbsp   Bona olive oil
- 130   ml   Vegetable broth

- 1   prize   salt
- 1   prize   pepper
- 4th   Spr   Lemons (juice)

time

35 min. Total time 20 min preparation time 15 min.cooking & resting time

preparation

Finely chop the peeled onion and roughly chop the basil leaves.

Wash the salmon, pat dry, season with salt and lemon juice on all sides.

Heat the oil in a pan and fry the salmon steak on both sides for 5 minutes. Put the onion cubes in the pan and fry them. Add the tomatoes and deglaze with the vegetable stock, cook briefly. Season with salt and pepper and sprinkle with the basil leaves.

CLASSIC CUCUMBER SALAD

Ingredients for 4 servings

- 2 Pc Cucumber
- 1 Pc onion
- 15th G sugar
- 1 TL salt
- 4th Tbsp Bona oil
- 4th Tbsp vinegar

time

25 min. Total time 15 min preparation time 10 min.cooking & resting time

preparation

Wash the cucumber and cut into slices. Peel the onion and cut into rings.

Mix all ingredients and season again. Let it steep for 10 minutes.

SUGAR SNAP

Ingredients for 4 servings

- 400 G sugar snap
- 1 prize salt
- 1 TL butter

time

10 min. Total time 10 min preparation time

preparation

Rinse and dab the sugar snap peas briefly. Heat the butter in a pan and toss the snow peas in it for a few minutes. Salt to taste and serve.

CLASSIC CUCUMBER SALAD

Ingredients for 4 servings

- 2 Pc Cucumber
- 1 Pc onion
- 15th G sugar
- 1 TL salt
- 4th Tbsp Bona oil
- 4th Tbsp vinegar

time

25 min. Total time 15 min preparation time 10 min.cooking & resting time

preparation

Wash the cucumber and cut into slices. Peel the onion and cut into rings.

Mix all ingredients and season again. Let it steep for 10 minutes.

VEGAN BREAD DUMPLINGS

Ingredients for 2 servings

- 300 G Bread rolls (vegan and dry)
- 180 ml soy milk
- 2 Tbsp Parsley (chopped)
- 1 Pc Onion (small, chopped)
- 2 Tbsp Bona olive oil
- 3rd Tbsp Soy flour
- 1 prize nutmeg
- 1 TL salt

time

50 min. Total time 10 min preparation time 40 min.cooking & resting time

preparation

Heat 1 tablespoon of olive oil in a pan and lightly roast the onion in it.

Cut the rolls into small cubes and place in a bowl, add 1 tablespoon of olive oil, soy milk, soy flour, a pinch of nutmeg and salt - let the mixture swell for 5 minutes.

Add the onion pieces and the chopped parsley to the dumpling mixture and knead well - let the mixture stand for 20 minutes.

Bring plenty of salted water to the boil in a saucepan. In the meantime, form 6 dumplings of the same size with wet hands (the dumplings must have a smooth surface, otherwise they would disintegrate during cooking, i.e. you may re-form the dumplings with wet hands).

Soak the dumplings in the boiling water and let them steep for about 15 minutes on a low heat (the water must not boil), lift the dumplings out of the water and serve while hot.

RICE SOUP

Ingredients for 4 servings

- 1.25   l   Vegetable broth
- 1   prize   salt
- 0.5   Federation   chives
- 50   G   rice
- 1   Pc   egg

time

30 min. Total time 10 min preparation time 20 min.cooking & resting time

preparation

Wash the rice thoroughly. Bring the broth to a boil and stir in the rice.

Cook over a moderate heat for about 20 minutes, do not cover and stir every now and then. At the end of the cooking time, season with salt.

Wash the chives and cut into rolls with the scissors. Stir the egg into the soup and sprinkle with chives.

ZUCCHINI NOODLES

Ingredients for 2 servings

- 2 Pc zucchini
- 2 Tbsp Bona oil
- 1 prize salt
- 1 prize pepper
- 1 Tbsp Parsley, finely chopped
- 1 Pc lime

time

15 min. Total time 10 min preparation time 5 min. cooking & resting time

preparation

For our homemade zucchini noodles, first wash the zucchini and cut off both ends.

Then cut or turn the zucchini into fine, elongated strips with a spiral cutter or a slicer.

Now heat a saucepan with a dash of oil and sauté the zucchini noodles in it until firm to the bite for about 3-5 minutes - turning or stirring occasionally.

Season with salt and pepper to taste and add a dash of lime juice - garnish with parsley and the perfect low-carb zucchini noodles are ready.

ZUCCHINI - POTATO CASSEROLE

Ingredients for 4 servings

- 4th   Pc   zucchini
- 4th   Pc   Potatoes
- 3rd   Pc   tomatoes
- Parsley
- 4th   Pc   Garlic cloves
- 1   prize coriander
- 5   Tbsp   Bona oil
- 1   prize pepper
- 1   prize salt

time

40 min. Total time 10 min preparation time 30 min.cooking & resting time

preparation

Peel the potatoes, cut them into slices and briefly bring to the boil in boiling water.

Dice the tomatoes and slice the zucchini.

Spread some oil in an ovenproof dish. Layer the potato slices, the diced tomatoes and the zucchini slices in it.

Season each layer with salt, pepper, garlic, coriander and parsley.

Put a little oil on the top layer.

Cover with aluminum foil or a lid and cook in the oven at 200 ° C for about 30 minutes.

POTATOES FROM THE STEAMER

Ingredients for 4 servings

1 kg Potatoes

1 prize salt

time

45 min. Total time 10 min preparation time 35 min.cooking & resting time

preparation

Peel and dice the potatoes and place in the perforated steamer. Season with salt and bay leaf and steam for approx. 15 minutes.

Excellent as a side dish and quickly prepared in the steamer.

TZATZIKI

Ingredients for 8 servings

- 1   kg   Yoghurt (at least 3.2%)
- 1   Pc   Cucumber (large)
- 4th   Pc   Garlic cloves, pressed
- 2   Tbsp   Bona olive oil
- 3rd   prize salt
- 1   prize pepper
- 1   Tbsp   Parsley, chopped

time

30 min. Total time 30 min preparation time

preparation

For the tsatsiki, first drain the yogurt overnight in a sieve (covered with a tea towel). Vigorously stir in the olive oil.

Coarsely grate the cucumber, squeeze it out and add to the yoghurt.

Season to taste with crushed garlic, salt, pepper and parsley.

Place in the refrigerator for at least 1 hour.

KOHLRABI SALAD WITH APPLES

Ingredients for 4 servings

- 0.5   cups   Schärdinger Berghof sour cream
- 1   Pc   onion
- 0.5   Federation   parsley
- 1   Pc   Lemons (juice)
- 1   Tbsp   honey
- 800   G   Kohlrabi
- 2   Pc   Apples
- 1   prize   pepper
- 1   prize   salt

time

15 min. Total time 15 min preparation time

preparation

Peel the apples and kohlrabi and grate finely. Peel onions and cut them into fine pieces.

Wash, drain and chop the parsley.

Mix lemon juice, honey, salt, pepper and sour cream into a dressing.

Pour the sauce over the salad and mix well.

RASPBERRY SMOOTHIE

Ingredients for 1 serving

- 100   ml   milk
- 120   G   Raspberries
- 75   G   Yogurt (low fat)
- 1   TL   vanilla sugar
- 2   Pc   Mint leaves

time

10 min. Total time 10 min preparation time

preparation

Mix the fresh raspberries finely with a hand blender.

Then milk, low-fat yogurt and vanilla sugar are mixed with the pureed raspberries and poured into a decorative glass.

The finished raspberry smoothie is garnished with the remaining raspberries and a leaf of fresh mint.

FRIED CHANTERELLES

Ingredients for 1 serving

- 100   G   Chanterelles
- 1   TL   Bona oil
- 1   Pc   Shallots (finely chopped)
- 3rd   Tbsp   Parsley (chopped)
- 0.5   Tbsp   butter
- 1   prize salt
- 1   prize pepper

time

15 min. Total time 10 min preparation time 5 min.cooking & resting time

preparation

For the fried chanterelles, first clean, dice or finely cut the shallot.

Then fry the cleaned chanterelles and shallot in a pan with a dash of oil. This creates a lot of liquid. Steam until the liquid has completely evaporated.

Then add the chopped parsley, salt and freshly ground pepper or season with it.

Refine the fried chanterelles with a piece of butter in the pan and serve.

CAULIFLOWER CASSEROLE

Ingredients for 4 servings

- 250   G   Schärdinger Berghof sour cream
- 150   G   Grated cheese
- 1   Tbsp   Margarine (for greasing)
- 2   Pc   Eggs
- 0.5   kg   Potatoes
- 1   Pc   cauliflower
- 1   shot   milk
- 60   G   Breadcrumbs
- 1   prize pepper
- 1   prize salt

time

50 min. Total time 30 min preparation time 20 min. cooking & resting time

preparation

Divide the cauliflower into florets and cook in a saucepan as large as possible for about 8 minutes in salted water with a dash of milk. First add the cauliflower to the boiling water otherwise it will get mushy.

Boil the potatoes with the skin in salted water until al dente and then peel them while hot.

Grease the casserole dish well and alternate potatoes, cut into slices and layer cauliflower.

Separate eggs, beat snow. Mix the yolks with the sour cream. Season with a pinch of salt and pepper. Fold in the snow and grated cheese.

Pour the mixture over the cauliflower and potatoes. Scatter some cheese and breadcrumbs on top.

Bake in the preheated oven at 200 degrees for about 20 minutes.

BREADED ZUCCHINI

Ingredients for 4 servings

- 2 Pc zucchini
- 1 prize salt
- 1 prize pepper
- 80 G Flour
- 80 G Crumbs
- 2 Pc Eggs
- 3rd Tbsp Bona oil

time

30 min. Total time 10 min preparation time 20 min.cooking & resting time

preparation

Wash the zucchini well, cut off the ends and cut the vegetables lengthways into approx. 4 equal slices and season with salt and pepper on both sides.

Prepare flour for the breadcrumbs in a plate. In another plate, whisk the eggs, stir in a dash of milk and season with salt. Arrange a third plate with breadcrumbs.

First turn the courgettes in the flour, then dip them in the egg mixture and then roll them in the breadcrumbs.

Bake the breaded zucchini in hot fat until golden brown on both sides.

RATATOUILLE

Ingredients for 2 servings

- 2   Pc   zucchini
- 1   Pc   Melanzani
- 3rd   Pc   Paprika (red / green / yellow)
- 1   Pc   Vegetable onion
- 5   Pc   Pepperoni
- 2   Tbsp   Bona olive oil
- 400   G   Tomatoes (diced)
- 2   Tbsp   soy sauce
- 1   prize   salt
- 1   prize   pepper
- 1   prize   Curry spice mix
- 1   prize   oregano
- 1   prize   basil

time

45 min. Total time 20 min preparation time 25 min.cooking & resting time

preparation

Cut the zucchini into cubes. Cut the aubergine into cubes with the black skin.

Core 1 green, red and yellow pepper each and cut into bite-sized pieces.

Peel the vegetable onion (or 2-3 other onions) and cut into crescents (so cut once and then cut the halves into slices).

Cut the pepperoni and zucchini into wafer-thin slices. Dice all vegetables, place in a high pan (or saucepan) and cook with 1-2 tablespoons of olive oil for 5-10 minutes (depending on how crispy you want it).

Wash the tomatoes and finely dice them. Then add the diced tomatoes and let everything simmer for about 5-10 minutes.

Season to taste with salt, pepper, 1-2 tablespoons soy sauce, possibly curry, if available cumin (cumin), if available Tabasco sauce and / or sambal oelek.

Arrange the ratatouille nicely in a bowl.

PUMPKIN SPAETZLE

Ingredients for 4 servings

- 2 Pc Eggs
- 100 G wheat flour
- 100 G Spelled flour
- 100 G pumpkin
- 1 prize salt
- 1 prize nutmeg
- 2 Tbsp butter
- 50 ml milk

time

30 min. Total time 10 min preparation time 20 min.cooking & resting time

preparation

Whisk eggs and milk, add flour, season with salt and nutmeg.

Peel and finely grate the pumpkin, add to the batter and stir well. (If the mixture is too runny, use more flour, if the mixture is too firm, add more milk or a dash of water.)

Bring the water to the boil with a little salt. Press the mixture through a spaetzle sieve, bring to the boil briefly and rinse in cold water. Sieve the spaetzle and toss in a pan with melted butter.

STYRIAN AVOCADO SPREAD

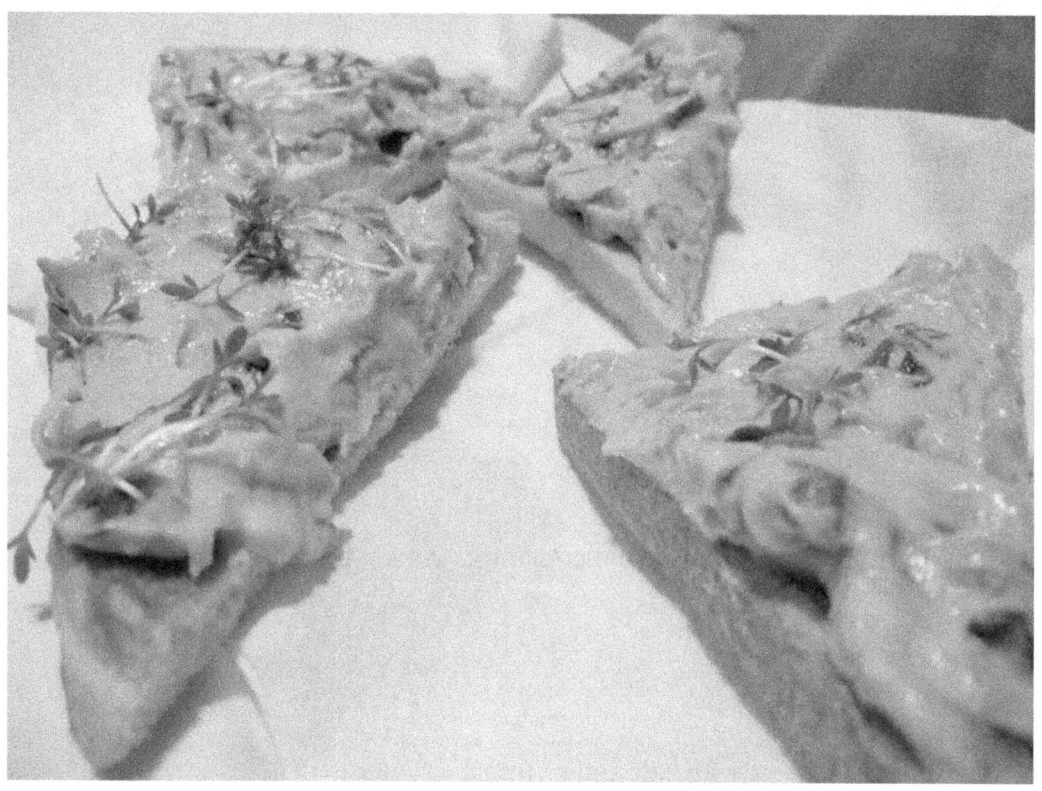

Ingredients for 6 servings

- 1   Pc   Fresh avocado
- 100   G   Curd
- 50   G   Dried tomatoes
- 1   Tbsp   Fresh cress
- 1   prize Cane sugar
- 2   cl   Pine vinegar or lemon juice
- 1   Tbsp   Pumpkin seeds
- 1   Pc   Shallot

time

10 min. Total time 10 min preparation time

preparation

Halve the avocado, first remove the stone and then the pulp with a spoon and place in a bowl.

Then pour stone pine vinegar or lemon juice over it and puree with a hand blender.

Then finely dice the shallot and tomatoes, cut the cress, finely chop the pumpkin seeds and add everything and mix with the remaining ingredients.

PIKEPERCH FILLET WITH VEGETABLES

Ingredients for 4 servings

- 4th   Pc   Pikeperch fillets
- 1   Pc   carrot
- 4th   Pc   spring onions
- 0.5   Federation   parsley smooth
- 4th   Tbsp   dry white wine
- 1   prize   salt
- 1   prize   black pepper
- 1   Tbsp   Flour

- 4th TL Bona olive oil
- 1 Pc Paprika (green)

100 G Celery (in fine strips)

Ingredients for the butter foam

- 1 Pc egg yolk
- 1 shot White wine
- 1 Tbsp butter

time

35 min. Total time 20 min preparation time 15 min.cooking & resting time

preparation

Wash the fish fillets, pat dry and drizzle with a little white wine. Season with salt and dust with flour on both sides.

Peel the carrot and cut into fine strips or slice. Wash the spring onions and cut into thin rings.

Wash and clean the celery and cut or slice into fine strips. Wash the peppers, remove the core and cut into fine strips.

Heat a little olive oil in a pan and fry the fish on both sides over a medium heat. Take out and keep warm - best in the oven at approx. 100 degrees wrapped in aluminum foil or covered.

Heat some more oil in the pan, sauté the onion, carrot pieces, celery and paprika in it for about 5 minutes and season with salt, pepper and parsley.

For the butter foam, beat the egg yolks with the white wine over a water bath until thick or foamy. Remove from heat and pour in the butter while stirring constantly.

SIMPLE PUMPKIN SOUP

Ingredients for 4 servings

- 2   Tbsp   butter
- 1   prize   Curry powder
- 2   Tbsp   fine millet flour
- 1   prize   freshly grated ginger
- 1   l   Vegetable broth
- 400   G   Pumpkin meat (diced small)
- 200   G   Carrots (diced small)
- 1   prize   Pepper and slaz
- 2   Tbsp   Whipped cream or crème fraîche
- 1   Pc   Onion (diced)

time

25 min. Total time 15 min preparation time 10 min.cooking & resting time

preparation

For the pumpkin soup, sauté the onion in butter until translucent, add the pumpkin and carrot cubes and sweat them too.

Sprinkle in the curry powder and millet flour and sauté.

Pour in the cold vegetable stock (clear vegetable soup) and bring to the boil while stirring, let the soup cook on a low flame for about 10 minutes, then puree.

Season to taste with ginger, pepper and salt. Refine with whipped cream if necessary.

VITAL SALAD

Ingredients for 4 servings

- 1   Can   Corn
- 6th   Pc   Cocktail tomatoes
- 1   Pc   endive salad
- 2   Pc   carrot

- 1   Pc   Cucumber
- 1   kg   Turkey meat
- 1   Tbsp   Paprika powder
- 1   shot   Bona olive oil

Ingredients for the dressing

- 1   shot   Bona olive oil
- 4th Tbsp   yogurt
- 1   TL   mustard
- 2   Tbsp   Balsamic vinegar

time

50 min. Total time 25 min preparation time 25 min.cooking & resting time

preparation

Wash and pick the lettuce. Grate the carrot into fine strips, cut the cucumber into slices. Quarter the tomatoes and take the corn out of the tin and rinse with cold water.

Mix the dressing of yogurt, olive oil, mustard and balsamic vinegar in a bowl and let it steep. (approx. 20-30 min.)

Meanwhile, cut the meat into strips, season with salt and pepper and season with a pinch of red paprika powder.

Heat the olive oil in a pan and fry the meat for a few minutes.

Arrange the lettuce leaves on plates, place the cut vegetables on top and pour the dressing over them. Just put the meat on the salad and serve with white bread.

COLESLAW

Ingredients for 4 servings

- 350 G White cabbage
- 3rd Pc Carrots
- 1 TL salt
- 1 prize pepper
- 1 TL Caraway seed

Ingredients for the marinade

- 3rd Tbsp Bona oil
- 2 Tbsp vinegar
- 1 prize sugar
- 1 prize salt
- 1 TL Mustard medium hot

time

120 min. Total time 30 min preparation time 90 min.cooking & resting time

preparation

Clean and finely slice the white cabbage. Wash in a colander and drain. Peel the carrots and slice them into pens. Mix the cabbage and carrots, season with salt and stir well. Let it steep for 1 hour.

Mix the oil, vinegar, mustard, sugar, pepper and salt to a marinade.

Squeeze out the cabbage and carrots, discard the resulting liquid. Pour the marinade over the cabbage and carrots, mix well and sprinkle with caraway seeds. Let it steep for another 0.5 hour.

STINGING NETTLE SPINACH

Ingredients for 4 servings

- 600 G Stinging nettle (upper part)
- 1 Pc onion
- 1 prize salt
- 1 prize pepper
- 0.5 Cup Whipped cream

- 1   Tbsp   butter

time

15 min. Total time 10 min preparation time 5 min.cooking & resting time

preparation

Put the nettles in a bowl and pour boiling water over them. Pour into the sieve and drain.

Peel the onion and cut into fine cubes. Melt the butter in a saucepan and sauté the onion cubes until translucent.

Cut the nettles into fine strips and stir into the onions. Salt and pepper and steam for a good 10 minutes, stirring occasionally.

Chop everything up with the hand blender and refine with cream.

TURKEY ROULADE

Ingredients for 4 servings

- 1   shot   Bona oil
- 4th   Schb   Cheese (Gouda or Emmentaler)

- 8th   Schb   ham
- 120   ml   Soup (clear)
- 1   kg   Turkey breast
- 1   Pc   onion
- 1   prize   pepper
- 1   prize   salt

time

50 min. Total time 30 min preparation time 20 min.cooking & resting time

preparation

For the turkey roulades, first season the turkey schnitzel with salt and pepper. Cover half of each with ham and cheese. Roll it up carefully and fix it with a toothpick.

Let the oil get hot in a frying pan and fry the turkey roulades in it, remove from the pan and roast the finely chopped onion. Pour the soup on top, add the turkey roulades and simmer everything on a small tray for 20-30 minutes.

Then take it out of the pan, portion it on plates and pour the gravy over it.

ZUCCHINI SOUP

Ingredients for 4 servings

- 2 Pc Zucchini (depending on size)
- 1 cups creme fraiche Cheese
- 50 G grated Emmental cheese
- 1 shot White wine
- 1 Pc Vegetable stock cubes
- 1 prize nutmeg
- 1 prize pepper
- 1 prize salt

time

35 min. Total time 15 min preparation time 20 min.cooking & resting time

preparation

Remove the two ends of the zucchini. Peel the zucchini, cut into cubes and cook in salted water for about 10 minutes. Then everything is pureed.

Add the creme fraiche, cheese and white wine to the soup. Season to taste with pepper, salt, nutmeg and vegetable stock cubes. Let simmer again for about 10 minutes on a medium flame.

Sprinkle with chives before serving.

PASTA WITH GREEN ASPARAGUS AND PROSCIUTTO

Ingredients for 4 servings

- 300 G Asparagus (green)
- 2 Pc Shallots
- 50 G butter
- 200 ml Whipped cream
- 1 Tbsp Parmesan (grated)
- 8th Schb Prosciutto
- 125 ml Asparagus stock
- 1 prize salt
- 1 prize White pepper
- 400 G Penne

time

35 min. Total time 35 min preparation time

preparation

Wash the asparagus, cut away the dry ends. Peel the asparagus spears thinly in the lower third. Cook the asparagus in a little salted water for approx. 7 minutes until al dente, rinse in ice water and drain. Thirds the rods. Set aside the asparagus stock for the sauce.

Dice shallots and sauté in butter until lightly. Pour in the asparagus stock. Pour in the cream and cook for approx. 2 minutes. Puree the sauce and strain it through a sieve.

At the same time, cook the penne (tubular noodles) in salted water until al dente, strain and drain briefly.

Heat the sauce, briefly heat the asparagus in it. Mix the parmesan with the asparagus sauce. Garnish with thin slices of prosciutto (Parma ham).

CELERY CREAM SOUP

Ingredients for 4 servings

- 1   l   Beef soup
- 0.5 kg   celery
- 1   Tbsp Bona oil

- 1   Pc   Lemon (juice)
- 1   Pc   onion
- 2   Pc   Garlic cloves, pressed
- 1   prize   pepper
- 1   prize   salt
- 0.5   cups   Schärdinger Berghof sour cream

time

25 min. Total time 10 min preparation time 15 min.cooking & resting time

preparation

Dice the celery and drizzle with lemon juice to prevent it from turning brown. Peel and finely chop the onion and sauté in oil. Add the squeezed garlic and celery pieces.

Roast everything briefly, pour on the soup and simmer on a low flame for about 15 minutes, then puree the soup with a hand blender. Mix in the sour cream and season everything with the spices.

FRIED RICE

Ingredients for 4 servings

- 250   G   Rice (e.g. long grain rice)

- 1 shot Peanut oil for the pan
- 1 shot light soy sauce
- 500 ml water

time

60 min. Total time 5 min preparation time 55 min.cooking & resting time

preparation

Wash rice thoroughly and soak in cold water for about 1/2 hour. Then drain and add to boiling water.

When it is half cooked, take it off the hob, drain it and let it cool down.

Heat the oil in a pan and fry the rice in it until it is golden yellow. Always stir well. Pour in the soy sauce and stir well.

Remove the fried rice from the hob and serve.

CHICKEN WITH STIR-FRIED VEGETABLES IN SOY SAUCE

Ingredients for 2 servings

- 300   G   Chicken (sliced)
- 100   G   broccoli
- 1   Pc   carrot
- 1   Kn   Onion (red)
- 150   G   Bean sprouts
- 1   Pc   paprika
- 2   Tbsp   soy sauce
- 2   Tbsp   Oyster sauce
- 1   Kn   garlic
- 2   Tbsp   peanut oil

time

15 min. Total time 10 min preparation time 5 min.cooking & resting time

preparation

Chop the vegetables including the onion and garlic. Sear the chicken in 2 tablespoons of peanut oil. When the meat is seared all over, remove it from the pan.

Now add the vegetables and garlic to the pan and fry for 2-3 minutes. Deglaze with a few tablespoons of water and add the soy sauce.

Fry the vegetables for another 2 minutes and then add the meat again. Fry everything again for a good 2 minutes while stirring and season with the oyster sauce.

EGG SOUP

Ingredients for 2 servings

- 750 ml chicken broth
- 2 Pc Eggs
- 1 prize Salt (to taste)
- 1 prize parsley

time

15 min. Total time 15 min preparation time

preparation

Bring the chicken broth to the boil. Whisk the eggs and stir quickly into the hot broth. Bring to the boil for 2 minutes while stirring.

PEA PUREE

Ingredients for 4 servings

- 0.5 kg Peas (firsch or TK)
- 1 Tbsp butter
- 1 prize salt
- 1 prize pepper

time

30 min. Total time 10 min preparation time 20 min.cooking & resting time

preparation

For the pea puree, salt water is brought to the boil in a saucepan and the peas are boiled in it until soft - then strain the saucepan and strain the peas.

Heat the butter in a pan and fry the peas in it, stirring constantly. Season to taste with salt and pepper.

MEDITERRANEAN PASTA SALAD WITH OLIVE DRESSING

Ingredients for 4 servings

- 250   G   Spiral pasta
- 1   Pc   Red pepper
- 1   Pc   yellow or green peppers

- 1   Tbsp   Bona oil
- 2   Tbsp   Bona olive oil
- 2   Pc   Cloves of garlic, crushed
- 1   Pc   Eggplant, diced
- 2   Pc   Zuccini, cut into thick slices
- 2   Pc   large tomatoes, peeled, without seeds
- 5   Tbsp   flat-leaf parsley, chopped
- 1   TL   freshly ground black pepper
- 150   G   Feta cheese, crumbled

Ingredients for the olive dressing

- 2   Tbsp   Balsamic vinegar
- 6th   Pc   Olives (black)
- 125   ml   Bona olive oil
- 1   prize   pepper
- 1   prize   salt

time

55 min. Total time 30 min preparation time 25 min.cooking & resting time

preparation

Put the spiral pasta in a large saucepan with boiling water and cook for 10-12 minutes until al dente. Drain, spread out in a layer on a baking sheet and let dry. Chill without the lid.

Halve the red and yellow peppers lengthways. Remove seeds and whites. Cut the bell pepper into large pieces. Place with the cut side down under the preheated oven grill and brown until the skin blisters. Let cool under a kitchen towel or in a transparent bag, peel off the skin and discard. Cut the paprika meat into thick strips.

Heat the sunflower and olive oil in a pan. Add the garlic and aubergine and brown quickly, turning constantly. Remove from heat and pour into a large bowl. Steam the zucchini for 1-2 minutes until they are firm to the bite. Rinse under cold water, drain and add to the aubergine pieces.

Olive dressing: 6 large black olives, pitted, 125 ml olive oil, 2 tablespoons balsamic vinegar, salt, freshly ground black pepper. Chop the olives in the food processor. Slowly pour in olive oil and continue processing until a smooth mass is formed. Add vinegar, season with salt and freshly ground black pepper and stir until smooth.

Mix the pasta, bell pepper, aubergine, zucchini, tomatoes, parsley and pepper in a large bowl. Arrange on serving plates, pour the feta cheese over them and drizzle with the dressing.

INDIAN LENTIL STEW

Ingredients for 4 servings

- 3rd   Pc   tomatoes
- 1   TL   Mustard seeds
- 1   prize   salt
- 1   prize   pepper
- 2   Pc   paprika
- 250   G   Red lenses
- 200   ml   Coconut milk
- 2   Pc   Garlic cloves

- 2   Pc   Medium sized potatoes
- 450   ml   clear vegetable soup
- 1   Pc   Onion, great
- 2   TL   curry
- 1   shot   Bona oil
- 1   Pc   Ginger (approx. 2cm)

time

55 min. Total time 30 min preparation time 25 min.cooking & resting time

preparation

For this classic lentil dish, first peel and finely chop the garlic. Peel and chop the onion. Wash the bell pepper, remove the stem, core and cut into cubes. Peel the ginger as well and cut finely.

Wash the tomatoes, scratch the skin a little with a knife, pour hot water over them and rinse with cold water. Then peel the tomatoes and cut them into small cubes.

Peel the potatoes and cut into bite-sized pieces or cubes.

Now roast the curry powder together with the mustard seeds in a high pan. Then add a dash of oil, the finely chopped garlic and ginger and fry briefly.

Now add the lentils and the pepper pieces to the pan and fry them briefly, stirring constantly.

Then pour the clear vegetable soup on top and bring to the boil. Add the finely chopped tomato pieces, coconut milk and potatoes to the pan and simmer gently for about 20-25 minutes, until the lentils and potato pieces are soft.

Finally mix in the onion pieces and season well with salt and pepper.

STUFFED ZUCCHINI

Ingredients for 4 servings

- 2   Pc   small zucchini
- 50   G   White bread
- 50   G   Serrano ham, thin slices
- 2   Pc   Garlic cloves
- 50   G   Tetilla or Emmentaler
- 1   Pc   fresh egg
- 2   Tbsp   Parsley, chopped, smooth
- 1   prize salt
- 1   prize black pepper
- 3rd   Tbsp   Bona olive oil
- 25th   G   grated manchego

time

60 min. Total time 25 min preparation time 35 min.cooking & resting time

preparation

Wash and clean the zucchini, remove the stems, cut in half lengthways and remove the stones.

Soak the bread in warm water, squeeze it out and chop it finely. Cut the ham into fine strips. Peel the garlic and chop in to fine slithers. Chop the cheese into small cubes.

Preheat the oven to 200 ° C, circulating air, 170 ° C, gas mark 3-. Mix the bread, strips of ham, garlic, cheese cubes, egg and parsley together well. Salt and pepper the mixture and pour into the zucchini halves.

Grease a large baking dish with 1 tablespoon of olive oil, put the zucchini in it and sprinkle with the manchego. Drizzle with the rest of the oil. Baked the zucchini on the middle rack in the oven for about 35 minutes, then cut into pieces.

CHICKPEA AND ZUCCHINI PATTIES

Ingredients for 2 servings

- 1 Pc Zucchini (large)
- 1 Pc onion
- 100 G ham
- 1 Kn garlic
- 4th Bl parsley
- 300 G Chickpeas (canned, drained)
- 2 Tbsp Lemon juice
- 1 Tbsp Crumbs

time

150 min. Total time 30 min preparation time 120 min.cooking & resting time

preparation

Put the chickpeas in a tall container and then grind them finely with a hand blender. Grate the zucchinis and squeeze them firmly so that the water can drain off and then add to the chickpeas.

Chop the onion, garlic and parsley, dice the ham and add to the chickpea mixture and fold in the crumbs. Stir well and season with lemon juice, salt and pepper.

Shape the dough into 6 loaves and put them in the fridge for at least 2 hours. Then place on a baking sheet lined with baking paper.

Preheat the oven to 220 degrees hot air and then bake the patties for 10 minutes, turn and bake on the other side for another 10 minutes.

BAKED AUBERGINES (AUBERGINES)

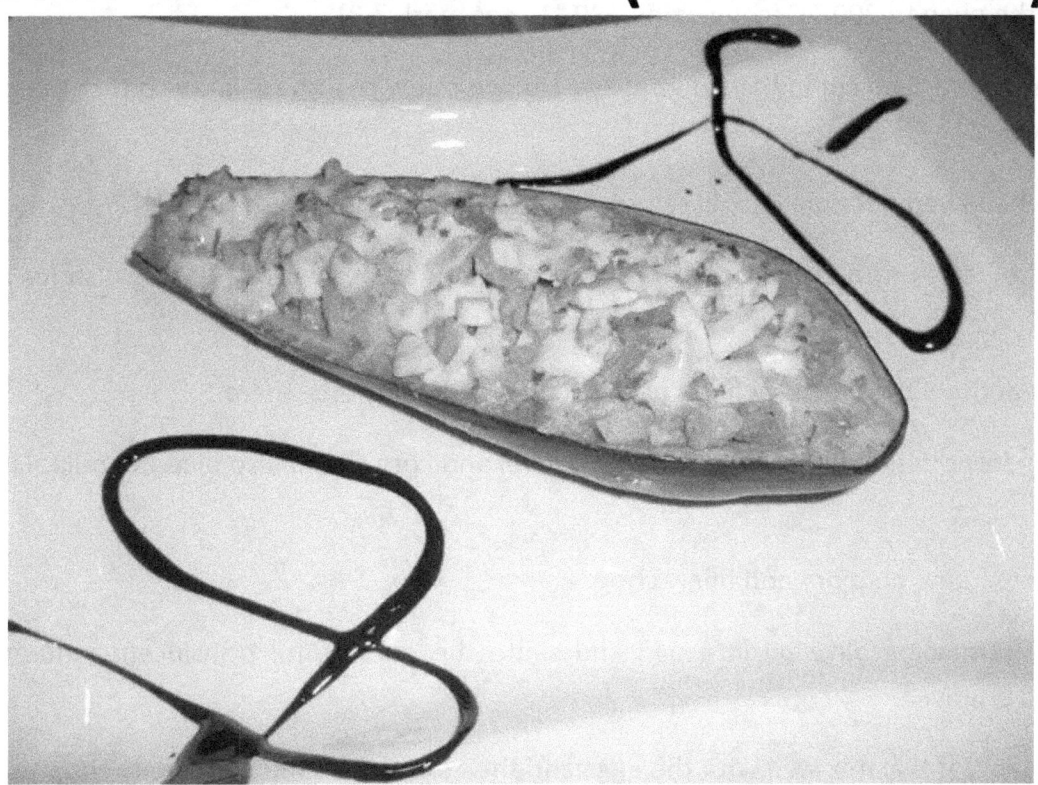

Ingredients for 2 servings

- 300   G   Eggplant (eggplant)
- 5   Tbsp   Bona olive oil
- 1   prize   salt
- 1   prize   pepper
- 2   Pc   Eggs
- 2   Pc   Beefsteak tomatoes
- 1   Pc   onion
- 0.5   Federation   parsley
- 100   G   Mozzarella
- 2   Tbsp   Pine nuts

time

50 min. Total time 40 min preparation time 10 min.cooking & resting time

preparation

Preheat the oven to 200 ° C (convection 180 ° C, gas mark 2-3).

Wash aubergines and cut in half lengthways. Hollow out with a sharp knife so that the fruit does not collapse.

Soak the hollowed out pulp in cold salted water for 10 minutes.

Spread the halves with 2 tablespoons of olive oil, salt and pepper in a baking dish for about 10 minutes.

In the meantime, boil the eggs hard, quench, peel and finely dice them.

Scald tomatoes with boiling water (blanch), peel and core them, also dice the pulp. Finely dice the onion.

Pat the aubergine pulp dry and finely chop.

Heat the remaining olive oil in a pan and sauté the onion until translucent, aubergine and tomatoes briefly.

Dice the mozzarella, mix well with the eggs and the contents of the pan, finely chop the parsley into the mixture, season everything and season to taste.

Spread on the pre-baked halves and bake again for about 15 minutes.

FRIED SALMON FILLETS

Ingredients for 4 servings

- 4th Pc Salmon fillet
- 1 Tbsp Fennel grains
- 1 Tbsp Peppercorns
- 1 prize sugar
- 1 TL coriander

time

45 min. Total time 15 min preparation time 30 min.cooking & resting time

preparation

Wash and dry the salmon fillets and make a cut on the skin side so that the fat can escape while frying.

Finely grind the spices in a mortar and rub them on the skin side of the fillets. Then let the fillets steep for about 30 minutes.

Then heat some oil in a pan and fry the fillets on the skin side. At the very end, turn the fillets and fry them briefly (approx. 1-2 minutes). Then arrange on plates and serve.

FRUIT SALAD FOR CHILDREN

Ingredients for 4 servings

- 4th   Pc   Bananas
- 250   G   Strawberries
- 100   G   blueberries
- 2   Pc   Apples
- 250   ml   orange juice
- 3rd   Pc   kiwi
- 0.5   Pc   Lemon (to drizzle)

time

15 min. Total time 15 min preparation time

preparation

Peel and slice the bananas. Quarter the apples, remove the core, peel and cut into small cubes. Remove the green from the strawberries, wash and cut into small pieces. Peel the kiwi and cut into small pieces.

Put everything in a bowl, squeeze the lemon and drizzle the fruit with it. Pour the orange juice over it, stir and serve.

NETTLE SOUP

Ingredients for 4 servings

- 4th   Pc   Stinging nettle shoots
- 1   prize   pepper
- 1   Pc   egg yolk
- 1   TL   parsley
- 1   Pc   Onion (small)
- 2   Tbsp   Flour
- 2   Tbsp   butter
- 300   ml   milk
- 750   ml   Chicken soup (clear)
- 1   prize   salt

time

45 min. Total time 20 min preparation time 25 min.cooking & resting time

preparation

Wash the nettles under cold water. Put the nettles in a saucepan and pour the hot soup over them and then cook on a low flame for about 10 minutes and strain - but collect the soup.

Peel and chop the onion. Whisk the egg yolks with 100 ml of water. Finely chop the parsley. Cut or puree the nettle very finely.

Sauté the finely chopped onion and parsley in butter and then add the flour.

Let everything sear briefly over a low flame while stirring - the flour should be light yellow - and then pour the rest of the cold milk over everything and stir until smooth.

Add the nettle stock and let it boil for 15 minutes, then add the nettles and briefly bring to the boil again.

Season to taste with salt and pepper and mix with the egg yolks whisked in milk.

OATMEAL MUESLI

Ingredients for 4 servings

- 200 G Apple
- 200 G Pears
- 50 G Nuts (chopped)
- 170 G oatmeal
- 0.5 l milk
- 2 Tbsp Lemon juice
- 1 Tbsp honey

time

15 min. Total time 15 min preparation time

preparation

Cut the fruit with the skin into small pieces. Mix with the nuts and oatmeal.

Pour the milk on top and add honey and lemon juice to taste.

GRILLED FENNEL

Ingredients for 4 servings

- 2   Pc   Fennel bulbs
- 2   Tbsp   Bona olive oil
- 1   prize   sea-salt
- 1   prize   Pepper (freshly ground)

time

14 min. Total time 10 min preparation time 4 min.cooking & resting time

preparation

The green stalks are cut off from the fennel. Cut the fennel into slices about 1/2 cm thick. Grill on both sides for 3-4 minutes over medium heat.

While grilling, brush the fennel a few times with olive oil. Season with sea salt and pepper just before serving.

GREEN ASPARAGUS AU GRATIN

Ingredients for 4 servings

- 500   G   green asparagus
- 2   Pc   Garlic cloves
- 120   ml   Bona olive oil
- 50   G   Breadcrumbs
- 40   G   Parmesan (freshly grated)
- 6th   Bl   basil
- 1   prize pepper
- 1   prize salt

time

35 min. Total time 10 min preparation time 25 min. cooking & resting time

preparation

Cut off about 1 cm from the asparagus ends, peel the stalks thinly up to the top third.

Put the asparagus in boiling salted water with a pinch of sugar and bring to the boil, remove from the heat and let it steep for 10 minutes - then lift the asparagus out of the water and drain on a tea towel.

Place the asparagus in an ovenproof dish or on an ovenproof plate and season with salt and pepper.

Peel the garlic and press through a garlic press - fry it in a pan with a dash of olive oil over medium heat and then stir in the breadcrumbs.

Spread the garlic and crumbs mixture on the asparagus and sprinkle with the parmesan.

Gratinate for 3-4 minutes under the grill on the 2nd shelf from the top.

CARROT AND ZUCCHINI FRITTERS

Ingredients for 4 servings

- 2   Pc   zucchini
- 500   G   Carrots
- 2   Spr   Lemon juice
- 4th   Tbsp   parsley
- 2   Pc   Eggs
- 2   Tbsp   oatmeal
- 1   Tbsp   Bona oil
- 1   prize   salt
- 1   prize   pepper

time

20 min. Total time 15 min preparation time 5 min.cooking & resting time

preparation

First the zucchini is washed and the ends removed and peeled. Peel the carrots and clean them too.

Roughly grate both with a grater and mix with lemon juice, parsley, egg and the oat flakes.

Then season with salt and pepper.

The oil is now heated in a pan. The vegetable mixture is spooned into the pan, flattened and seared until crispy. Turn several times. Drain on kitchen paper.

Serve on beautiful plates.

MILLET BREAKFAST

Ingredients for 4 servings

- 250 G millet
- 500 ml milk
- 2 Tbsp honey
- 2 Pc Apples
- 1 Tbsp Raisins
- 2 Tbsp Cranberries

time

30 min. Total time 10 min preparation time 20 min.cooking & resting time

preparation

Wash the millet with hot water - rinse in a colander and put in a saucepan. Add enough water to just cover the millet.

Cook over medium heat until the water has been completely absorbed by the millet.

Pour the milk over the millet and cook until it is soft. Sweeten with honey to taste and refine with the finely chopped apples, raisins and cranberries.

CLASSIC ASPARAGUS

Ingredients for 4 servings

- 2   kg   Asparagus (green or white)

- 12th Schb Ham (smoked)
- 12th Pc medium potatoes
- 4th Pc Eggs
- 1 prize salt
- 1 prize sugar
- 1 Tbsp butter

Ingredients for the sauce

- 200 G butter
- 2 Pc egg yolk
- 4th Tbsp White wine
- 1 Tbsp Lemon juice
- 1 prize salt
- 1 prize Pepper White)

time

40 min. Total time 20 min preparation time 20 min. cooking & resting time

preparation

Cook the peeled asparagus in plenty of hot water (seasoned with salt, sugar and butter) for 15-20 minutes until al dente.

Peel the potatoes and cook as usual. The eggs are hard-boiled.

For the sauce: Melt the butter in a saucepan and let cool down a little.

Beat the egg yolks with lemon juice and white wine over a hot water bath until the mixture is thick.

Then the cooled and melted butter is slowly beaten in. Now the sauce is seasoned with salt and pepper.

LINGUINE WITH ASPARAGUS

Ingredients for 4 servings

- 100   G   Shallots
- 500   G   Asparagus, green
- 2   Tbsp   butter
- 200   ml   Chicken soup, of course
- 300   G   Linguine (flat pasta)
- 200   G   Mascarpone
- 1   prize   salt
- 1   prize   black pepper
- 2   TL   chervil

time

40 min. Total time 30 min preparation time 10 min.cooking & resting time

preparation

First cut the shallots into small cubes. Wash the asparagus and cut off the lower ends.

Then peel the asparagus stalks in the lower third and cut diagonally into pieces about 1 cm wide (peel the whole stalks for white asparagus).

For the pasta, bring plenty of salted water to the boil and cook the linguine in bubbly salted water according to the package instructions.

In the meantime, froth the butter in a saucepan and fry the shallots in it until they are light golden yellow.

Briefly sauté the chopped asparagus spears (without the heads), deglaze with the chicken soup, season with salt, pepper and cover and simmer for 5 minutes over low heat.

Add the asparagus tips and mascarpone to the remaining asparagus and cook for another 3 minutes - season with salt and pepper.

Drain the cooked linguine to the bite and mix with the asparagus and mascarpone sauce and some coarsely chopped chervil

TOMATO SPREAD

Ingredients for 4 servings

- 4th   Pc   Tomatoes, ripe
- 200   G   Sunflower seeds
- 1   prize   salt
- 1   prize   pepper
- 1   Tbsp   Tomato paste
- 1   TL   Lemon juice
- 40   G   Olives, pitted

time

10 min. Total time 10 min preparation time

preparation

Halve the tomatoes, cut out the stem end in a wedge shape. Cut the tomatoes into large cubes.

Add the sunflower seeds, tomato paste and lemon juice and puree everything to a homogeneous mass.

Cut olives into fine cubes and fold in. Season everything with salt and pepper.

www.ingramcontent.com/pod-product-compliance
Lightning Source LLC
Chambersburg PA
CBHW080613100526
44585CB00035B/2404